The Optimal CoFounder Interview Guide

JULIA McNAMARA

Copyright © 2019 CoFounderworx

Contents

SECTION		PAGE
01	Big Data, Big Personalities and CoFounders That Love Them	4
02	Look in the Mirror, and then Look for Your CoFounder	12
03	The Optimal CoFounder Interview Guide Question Section	22

Introduction

In working with some local accelerators a few years ago, we discovered that 67% of the early stage companies failed within 3 years of launch, due to CoFounder tension and eventually conflict. While our efforts had focused heavily on getting the technology and funding right, we watched, in disbelief, as the relationships between CoFounders disintegrated into resentment, tension and then outright conflict or apathy. We didn't have the information or recommendations to assist or prevent these team meltdowns. My first instinct was to find research to help with these challenges for CoFounders and found little research-based information available. Our team felt this ultimate waste of time and money was easily preventable!!

This was the basis of our three-year CoFounder journey. From our vantage point, the resultant falling out among team members, was completely unnecessary and preventable. Currently, we have collected data from 4,500 CoFounders and feel very confident outlining the "success metrics" for Founding teams.

The "success metrics" for CoFounders include: leadership qualities, mindsets, values and interventions necessary for Founding team success. Our findings have been captured into our CoFounderFit™ leadership assessment. However, CoFounders still ask which qualities and questions to ask when evaluating a potential CoFounder or strengthening their existing relationship. That is what we have captured in this book. A million thank-you's to the wonderful people who help grow our body of knowledge on how to best identify the correct qualities critical to founding teams success. A special thank you goes out to Amy Giddon, Sarah Michaelson, Andrea Minkow, Tami McLaughlin, Lynn Gonsor, Joe Covey, Professors Yaron Prywes and Paul Johnson of Columbia Business School and Insight, Comcast Ventures and Singularity University. Your insights have provided provide tremendous benefit to the CoFounder community! I hope the guidance that follows provides potential and existing CoFounders much more clarity into your Founding team journey.

Much success on your endeavours!
Julia

01

Big Data, Big Personalities and CoFounders That Love Them

QUANTIFYING HUMAN CAPITAL ATTRIBUTES IN COFOUNDER MATCH-UPS

01 Big Data, Big Personalities and CoFounders That Love Them

WHY IS UNDERSTANDING YOUR COFOUNDER SO IMPORTANT?

Running a startup brings out the best and worst in people. There are many books and articles about how to create a team and the latest way to manage an organization, but not enough about personality on Founding Teams. A large percentage of startups fail due to inter-team conflict – not poor planning, but conflict between personalities that don't mesh. This friction is often highest among CoFounders, especially in a startup.

Removing this friction is essential in the era of "human capital." Thirty years ago, people in startups focused on the actual technology, how it worked and how it could be built. A decade later, they were trying to optimize the tech and the related business models to find ways to make money. But now it's the time for human capital, a kind of last frontier that needs to be optimized by finding the right person for a specific job. This is now easier to accomplish, thanks to new ways of looking at people and personalities through data measurements.

PREDICTING GOOD WORKING RELATIONSHIPS THROUGH PERSONALITY TESTING

Many CoFounder arrangements start based on gut instinct. The people involved are often successful, with Type A personalities and confidence in their decisions and instincts. They may initially meet at a networking gathering and impress each other with their shared enthusiasm for an idea.

Instinct can sometimes bring success, but it's tricky when CoFounder partnerships are based solely on gut instinct. Enthusiasm is great, but it's short-lived if you don't align on the core attributes and beliefs for a successful working partnership. Two people who know each other through professional circles and get along well in social settings might seem like good matches, but their CoFounder journey can just as easily end in discord.

Of course, achieving the optimal results from personality testing requires a suitable test. My company, **CoFounderWorx,** offers a different take on personality testing that's specifically geared toward CoFounder compatibility. It revolves around the most important indicators of successful pairings, including values, motivations and other psychological factors. These personality traits come together to score potential CoFounders, taking into account their value to the business, including how they might perform from an investor's and venture capitalist's viewpoint. Using the test can improve the success rates of a startup by identifying the people best suited as solo founders or CoFounders, pairing up those who are best aligned on areas critical to CoFounder success. This test is complementary to other assessments such as the MBTI, Hogan and Korn Ferry, and focuses on the top five areas critical for successful partnerships.

> The research that CoFounderWorx has conducted is the basis of an innovative CoFounder compatibility test and has uncovered several factors that can provide critical value to CoFounders seeking successful partnerships.

01 Big Data, Big Personalities and CoFounders That Love Them

BUT WHAT IF YOU CAN'T TAKE THE TEST? WHAT QUALITIES SHOULD YOU LOOK FOR AS YOU SEARCH FOR YOUR COFOUNDER.

STRONG PREDICTORS OF SUCCESS—OR DISASTER One predictor for success is simply whether the CoFounders have known each other for a long time and/or worked together previously. This exposure does not mean they'll automatically be compatible to run a startup together, but it at least improves the odds of an agreeable partnership. Most partnerships only look at this factor, but there are many others that contribute to success or failure.

Some entrepreneurs might come from the corporate world and are eager to pull in other successful corporate executives as CoFounders. However, personality assessments have uncovered certain traits executives tend to possess that don't mesh well with being a CoFounder. For example, the "tolerance of uncertainty" covers someone's multiple risk profiles. It measures not just financial risk, but also reputational risk, a metric that matters more to people as they get older. Successful executives with a lot of time and energy invested in their careers often have much lower tolerances for risk than the average startup CoFounder. Startup founders need to make decisions based on imperfect information and do things that aren't the "corporate way," especially in the company's early years. An operations executive with 20 years of experience might not have the personality needed to make the bold decisions. So, despite their previous successes, they aren't primed for the CoFounder role.

Personality testing can uncover several red flags to help founders avoid serious problems. One metric worthy of special mention is integrity. Starting a business with someone requires a blend of skill sets and personality traits, but a shared moral compass is also essential. Testing this trait requires looking at more than just honesty – it's an examination of how that person views the world. How far are they willing to bend the rules? Will they treat staff equitably in the pursuit of growth? This is one of the hardest attributes to measure with just gut instinct, as people often show their true colors under the stress of a startup. Personality testing that can quantify integrity helps CoFounders avoid one of the biggest risks: choosing someone who isn't aligned with your moral compass. It's a fundamental difference that will lead to disagreements, poor long-term planning, and usually disaster. In lieu of taking a personality test,

one should look at the targeted questions to probe integrity provided later in this book.

A TALE OF THREE FOUNDERS

A common scenario is a fledgling company that has three high-powered people involved, all super Type A. The upside is that they are all very hardworking. The downside is they are also pretty controlling and demanding. They all have a high need for visibility and recognition. Such traits often translate into business success, but the issue is how they'll function as CoFounders. Which one gets to be the CEO? And will the other two CoFounders unconsciously resent the decision and start undermining the CEO's direction? Many of these factors are operating under the surface. If the need for recognition is too strong among the CoFounders, then the focus stays on their personal accomplishments instead of the company.

Targeted interviewing and Personality testing can sort out people who have too much drive and a too-dominating personality. Startups survive when those involved can talk through the big decisions and combine different viewpoints.

01 Big Data, Big Personalities and CoFounders That Love Them

Overly dominating people can hurt the company's progress, because they're often unwilling to see other points of view and might even avoid sound decisions that don't originate with them.

With these three CoFounders, will the two who aren't CEO stay in their lane if their personalities drive them into every decision? This is challenging in a startup, as everyone needs to pitch in and tackle various tasks to move the company forward.

Bringing together CoFounders should involve much more than matching up skill sets. Take a CMO and CTO: Their knowledge may be complementary, but not if they're both domineering and they don't share a moral compass. Advanced personality testing should be a standard practice to help founders and venture capitalists get the most out of every CoFounder matchup.

SKILL SETS: COMPLEMENTARY AT FIRST

In the early days, it's best to have CoFounders with complementary, rather than overlapping, skill sets. The first step in finding someone with a complementary skill set is to figure out what your own strengths and weaknesses are. The most common CoFounder pairing we see early on is: CMO/CTO or "sales/technical". Many non- technical founders ask us if they should find a technical CoFounder right away.

We advise to "try before you buy" and enter into any type of partnership carefully and on a trial (3-6 month) basis before entering into something more formal. In addition, non- technical founders (especially) should hire third parties to help interview potential CoFounders for technical skills. Hiring bad engineers is one of the major reasons startups fail, according to research. Make sure to review portfolios, former deliverables and check references. There are several coding skills assessments, such as HackerRank, that every potential technical CoFounder should take. We recommend StrengthsFinder as a viable and affordable assessment for business CoFounders.

We advise every founder to conduct due diligence on their CoFounder, including, if nearing a longer-term contract, a background and credit check. While most people balk when we mention a credit check, it is good to know how your potential CoFounder handles money.

VALUES

While skill sets should be complementary, values should be the as close to identical as possible. Many people proclaim to know their values, but cannot immediately identify them or rank them. When your values are in conflict, it feels like a kick in the stomach. Our research shows that when people are aligned on values, their relationships have more successful outcomes.

Look in the Mirror, and then Look for Your CoFounder

MINDSETS TO MAXIMIZE REFLECTION AND PARTNERSHIP POTENTIAL

02

02 Look in the Mirror and then Look for Your CoFounder

MINDSET—Take responsibility for what you are getting yourself into. Many Founders forget that choosing their Business Partner is their most important business decision.

Finding the best CoFounder for you will require that you exercise some level of self awareness. Be honest about what qualities you are looking for. The quickest way to determine what you want is to actually complete and reflect on the findings and questions written later in this book. Although this process might seem time-consuming, nothing is more time-consuming than separating from a poorly matched CoFounder situation. Be honest with yourself. Before you meet with anyone, you have to have thought these through and written down your answers.

MINDSET—Be selective. Determine what you want and don't settle for less.
Define What You Want; Be Specific
The first thing you should do is write down what qualities you want in a Co-Founder. Most CoFounders just focus on technical skill sets and don't think about how they are going to interact with this person for the next x years. Therefore, it is important to identify the behavioral as well as the technical skill sets needed. Make sure you articulate on paper the specific skills, knowledge, ability, experience, etc. needed by the applicant to be Your CoFounder. This is an important decision; you have every right to ask these questions. If the person won't or is reluctant to answer them, ask why, nicely. But if they won't answer these questions over time, you might want to move on.

CATEGORIZE THE SKILL SETS

To make sure that you don't get too dazzled by this person's technical prowess or charisma, categorize skills sets into technical and behavioral and values. Technical skills refer to specific skills needed to fulfill the job role, such as UX design. Behavioral attributes refer to how the person needs to act in order to fulfill that task. (e.g. self-motivated).

Try assessing each of the position's essential functions in light of 4 basic questions.
1. What must an applicant **know**? (Knowledge - technical or other skills)
2. How should she **be**? (Behavioral – organized, exciting, light-hearted)
3. What must he or she **bring**? (eg what specific contributions will you make as a CoFounder)
4. Where does she want to **go**? (what are her plans for the future?)

PRIORITIZE THE SKILL SETS BEFOREHAND

Most people just write down the skill sets, but you have to also prioritize what you want. If you don't write down what you want, you are less likely to be ob-

02 Look in the Mirror and then Look for Your CoFounder

jective in an interview. We make an excel spreadsheet that lists all requirements ranked per the categories below.

Categorize your requirements according to:
- Must Have's: Critical /non-negotiable
- Preferred: Desired/but still negotiable
- Nice to Have's: Can be acquired on the job

MINDSET—Treat this as a Job Interview

Many CoFounders rush into partnerships for many reasons. They don't take the time to write down what they want and therefore take whomever comes. Many times their shared excitement over a project idea leads potential CoFounders to not probe other areas and therefore make assumptions. Just because someone went to an excellent school does not mean they will make a good partner for you. Also, just because they are someone else's "Ideal Cofounder" in person or on paper, does not mean they are yours.

The key to effective interviewing and hiring is the establishment of guidelines. By deciding upon the essential functions of the position, you will be able to better determine how well this potential CoFounder matches YOUR specific requirements.

Factors to consider include:
- Is the performance of the functions the main reason the CoFounded company exists? Talk through the importance of each CoFounder's skill sets and contributions
- How much time, money and other items will each person contribute to the organization?
- How much value to the organization does the candidate's prior experience contribute?
- In the beginning, this person will have to juggle many hats. Can he or she manage this?

Spend time on the items above. They matter over the long term and are often the core of many disputes.

DURING THE INTERVIEW

Founders spend countless, wasted hours, asking the wrong interview questions to determine the right job or culture fit in a candidate; many of them end up as mis-hires that hurt the bottom line.

> Ask questions and then be quiet and LISTEN. Many Founders might talk too much during the interview. Let the candidate do the talking and carry 80-85% of the conversation.

It is extremely important to listen and concentrate on what they are saying. Then ask questions for more clarity, to probe deeper or keep the candidate on track. Ask only questions that are directly related to the job. These information gathering/problem solving questions like the ones below will help you collect vital information on potential CoFounders.

www.cofounderworx.com | **17**

Several types of questions are useful:
- **Open ended questions** are important because they often reveal attitudes and feelings, which need to be aligned in CoFounder relationships. These questions produce unexpected and valuable information, AND indicate how quickly a potential CoFounder can think on his feet. Example: "Tell me (more) about your job at Google..."
- **Behavioral questions** require a potential CoFounder to specifically analyze a situation and provide can provide specific examples to reveal the extent of their experience. Example: You said that you have a lot of experience managing people. What was the worst conflict situation you ever had with an employee and how did you diffuse that situation?
- **Direct questions** are more likely to yield concise answers and specific information. Example: "Why would you like to help me found this company?"
- **Probing questions** such as "Could you explain what you mean by...?" can further eliminate vagueness and clarify the candidate's views. Don't be afraid to use these types of questions to get to the root of the answer they're looking for.

After asking these questions, be quiet! This is difficult for many CoFounders. If you speak, you will seem over anxious. If you speak, you may influence the candidate's answers

BE MINDFUL OF YOUR QUESTIONS

Formulate questions that indicate whether or not a candidate meets the requirements you have established for the position. Keep three rules in mind:

1. Ask questions that focus on past employment performance. Avoid questions that address the candidate's personal lifestyles or habits.
2. Ask questions that relate to your listed skill, ability, knowledge or experience requirements.
3. Ask the same questions of all candidates.

02 Look in the Mirror and then Look for Your CoFounder

Avoid:
- Closed questions that require merely a yes or no response.
- Questions that are not dealing with areas that are not factors for job performance, such as gender, religion, disability and marital status.

CHOOSE AN OBJECTIVE THIRD PARTY

We suggest CoFounders consult an objective third party up to help CoFounders make decisions. Make sure you pick people who have a vested interested in the responsibilities of the position (to help you, not them or your future CoFounder).

Technical CoFounders pay attention here: many engineers bond over their technical skills and will feel very comfortable employing critical thinking about their potential CoFounder's "technical experience" but often feel uncomfortable really interacting and pushing on the "softer side".

Critical thinking is the process we use to reflect on, access and judge the assumptions underlying our own and others' ideas and actions. The more information we collect, the better.

UNDERSTANDING YOUR COFOUNDER THROUGH ACTIVE QUESTIONING

In the next section, we list the most powerful questions that guarantee to spark conversation with your CoFounder. In our work, we find it's very important to understand your CoFounder in many areas, but particularly the areas we listed below. Founders must go further than skill sets and ask about areas such as motivation, commitment and especially expectations about the business. The first year is great, but how about year 5? Our research shows that CoFounders who are aligned on the areas below have more successful CoFounder relationships.

The #1 quality that CoFounders request of their potential CoFounder is integrity. Our definition of integrity is personal accountability, tells the truth, and is willing to speak about shared Cofounder values, in order to intentionally create an ethical and transparent organizational culture. While it is good to

know if your potential CoFounder is honest, our work also shows that Co-Founder's definition of integrity varies, especially across cultures. While there are some "common denominators" of integrity such as people "following through on what they say" and "being honest".

> When one digs in, people differ on how much information to withhold or hold confidential, admitting mistakes versus blaming others, personal accountability, how much a CoFounder should put the organization's interests above its own.

We believe that the questions are meant as a discussion point and will uncover a lot of valuable information.

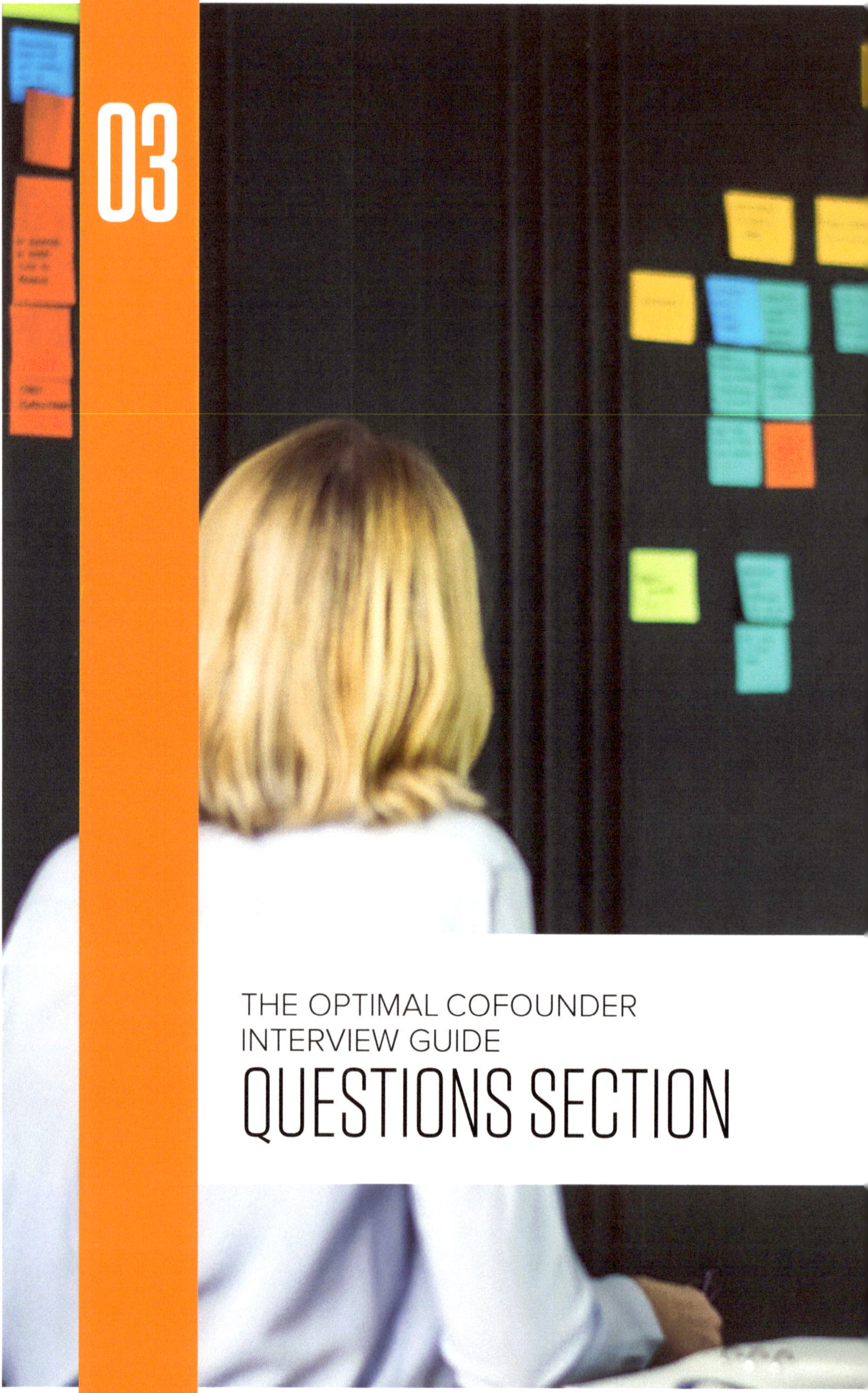

03

THE OPTIMAL COFOUNDER
INTERVIEW GUIDE
QUESTIONS SECTION

03 The Optimal CoFounder Interview Guide Questions Section

The following questions are meant as a starting point and will uncover a lot of valuable information. It might feel a little uncomfortable asking some of these questions, but nothing is more distressing than ending up in the wrong CoFounder relationship. Be brave.

Questions for:
- Understanding Your Cofounder
- Digging Deeper and Assessing
- Motivation
- Expectations
- Integrity
- Team Leadership

10 QUESTIONS TO UNDERSTAND YOUR COFOUNDER

It takes time, effort and compassion to understand your CoFounder. What people show us at first is not always who they are. It's not that people are being dishonest. Instead, these are many areas that people don't necessarily think about unless they are specifically asked. So, ask away and see what you find out! You both might be surprised at the answers. Also, be as honest as possible, or you will not attract the right CoFounder for you.

1. What element of our work attracted you to me (us)?

2. How would our company/work fit into your career goals?

3. Why do you think you would be a good "fit" for our company? With me?

4. What other life, other than career, goals do you have?

5. Describe the work environment or culture in which you thrive – most productive and happy.

6. Do you prefer working alone or as part of a team? Why?

7. Describe a project or idea (not necessarily your own) that was implemented, or carried out successfully, primarily because of your efforts.

8. How do you handle stress? Be specific.

9. Tell me about the support system you have set up for this entrepreneurial journey.

10. Have you ever had a CoFounder before? Can you tell me more about that relationship?

KEY POINTS TO LOOK FOR:
Interest and Culture Fit, Similar Life Goals, Stress Management.

03 The Optimal CoFounder Interview Guide Questions Section

10 QUESTIONS FOR ASSESSING MOTIVATION

These questions will provide tremendous insight into the level of drive, resiliency, and specific motivations. For example, if you are looking for a CoFounder that takes initiative, has a can-do attitude, the questions below can draw revealing answers.

1. What is the example of a perfect workday?

2. What is your philosophy on work vs play?

3. How would you describe ways you made your last role more effective?

4. What is the biggest setback you've ever had and how did you regain self-motivation?

5. What motivates you the most – money, altruism, achievement?

6. Can you describe a time when you recognized, due to an unmanageable workload, that you were unable to meet multiple deadlines. What did you do?

7. Every morning, how do you decide what's most important and why?

8. Do you think it's important for CoFounders to motivate each other? How?

9. If you didn't have to work, won the lottery, how would you spend your time?

10. Under what circumstances would you want to leave the company, shut it down or end the CoFounder relationship?

KEY POINTS TO LOOK FOR:
Primary Motivations and other Motivations, Energy Fit.

10 QUESTIONS FOR ASSESSING EXPECTATIONS

The questions below will provide tremendous insight into a potential Co-Founder's Expectations, particularly, the financial and time commitments required to be successful. Misalignment on Expectations often results in conflict.

1. Why were you drawn to this company?

2. Tell me about your financial expectations for Year 1? Year 5?

3. What do you like to do in your free time?

4. If this is your side hustle, under what circumstances will this become your full-time job?

5. If we were to become CoFounders, who will be the CEO?

6. If only one CoFounder is the face to the public, how do the other Co-Founders get recognition?

7. What criteria will make you relocate to pursue this opportunity?

8. If the company were to run out of money, what would you do?

9. Have you thought through the level of effort required to make this company successful?

10. How have you demonstrated commitment to a difficult goal before?

KEY POINTS TO LOOK FOR:
Alignment around Critical Company Elements, Level of Commitment

03 The Optimal CoFounder Interview Guide Questions Section

10 QUESTIONS FOR ASSESSING INTEGRITY

The #1 requested attribute for a CoFounder is integrity. However, definitions of integrity vary across cultures, so it's important for you to understand your definition of integrity, before finding a match. The questions below will provide tremendous insight into a broader definition of Integrity. For example, if you are someone that likes to move fast and bend the rules, you have to find a Co-Founder that is in alignment with your definition of Integrity.

1. Do you ascribe to a moral code in your life? What is your philosophy?

2. Have you ever been asked to "look the other way" for a colleague. If so, describe how you resolved the situation.

3. Have you ever been pressured by a family member or someone influential to do something? How did you handle it?

4. How have you handled situations when clients have been upset with your work?

5. Have you ever had to assert yourself and tell the truth despite a difficult outcome?

6. Describe a time that you were asked to bend the rules? What was the context? How did you feel about doing that?

7. What are your shortcomings or blindspots and how do you handle them?

8. Have you ever found a wallet on the street? What did you do?

9. Can you tell me about a time when you resolved an ethically challenged situation.?

10. How far would you go to save the company?

10 QUESTIONS FOR ASSESSING TEAM LEADERSHIP

The questions below will provide tremendous insight into how a potential Co-Founder's attitudes, approaches and methods towards collaboration, leadership and authority. For example, if you are looking for a CoFounder to help manage people, the questions below can draw revealing answers.

1. Have you ever started a company with other people?

2. How do you feel about titles and authority?

3. Can you tell me about a time you had to persuade a difficult team member to do something that wasn't aligned with his goals?

4. How do you keep yourself and others motivated?

5. What actions and behaviors of your current former team do you respond to most effectively?

6. Can you tell us about a time when something blew up at work, how did you handle it?

7. How do you feel about team members working remotely?

8. What methods do you use to hold people accountable?

9. When and how should team members make their own decisions?

10. How do you make sure all voices on the team are included?

KEY POINTS TO LOOK FOR:
Alignment on methods, openness and respect for others.

03 The Optimal CoFounder Interview Guide Questions Section

In summary, we don't want to overlook the importance of the human element in partnerships. While our efforts had focused heavily on getting the technology and funding right, we watched, in disbelief, as the relationships between CoFounders disintegrated into resentment, tension and then outright conflict or apathy. Our team felt this ultimate waste of time and money was easily preventable!

This was the basis of our three-year CoFounder journey. From our vantage point, the resultant falling out among team members, was completely unnecessary and preventable. Currently, we have collected data from 4,500 CoFounders and feel very confident outlining the "success metrics" for Founding teams.

The "success metrics" for CoFounders include: qualities, mindsets, values and interventions necessary for Founding team success. Our findings have been captured into our CoFounderFit™ leadership assessment. However, CoFounders are still asking me for what to look for when evaluating a potential CoFounder or strengthening their existing relationship. We hope this book provides you the research and language necessary to better assess potential CoFounders before partnering.

www.ingramcontent.com/pod-product-compliance
Lightning Source LLC
Chambersburg PA
CBHW040300220526
45473CB00002B/542